Cambridge **Discovery Education**™

▶ **INTERACTIVE READERS**

Series editor: Bob Hastings

ON THE MOVE
THE LIFE OF NOMADS

A2⁺

Genevieve Kocienda

CAMBRIDGE UNIVERSITY PRESS
Cambridge, New York, Melbourne, Madrid, Cape Town,
Singapore, São Paulo, Delhi, Mexico City

Cambridge University Press
32 Avenue of the Americas, New York, NY 10013-2473, USA

www.cambridge.org
Information on this title: www.cambridgev.org/9781107632936

© Cambridge University Press 2014

First published 2014

Printed in Hong Kong, China, by Golden Cup Printing Company Limited

A catalog record for this publication is available from the British Library.

Library of Congress Cataloging-in-Publication Data

Kocienda, G.
  On the move : the life of nomads : level A2+ / Genevieve Kocienda.
     pages cm. -- (Cambridge discovery interactive readers)
  ISBN 978-1-107-63293-6 (pbk. : alk. paper)
  1. Nomads--Juvenile literature. 2. Readers (Elementary) 3. English language--Textbooks for
foreign speakers. I. Title.

GN387.K644 2014
305.9'06918--dc23

                              2013018623

ISBN 978-1-107-632936

Additional resources for this publication at www.cambridge.org

Layout services, art direction, book design, and photo research: Q2ABillSMITH GROUP
Editorial services: Hyphen S.A.
Audio production: CityVox, New York
Video production: Q2ABillSMITH GROUP

Contents

Before You Read:
Get Ready!

How long have you lived in the same house? Most people live in the same house in the same town for many years. Maybe all their lives. But, some groups of people in the world move from place to place. They are called nomads.

Words to Know

Complete the sentences with the correct words.

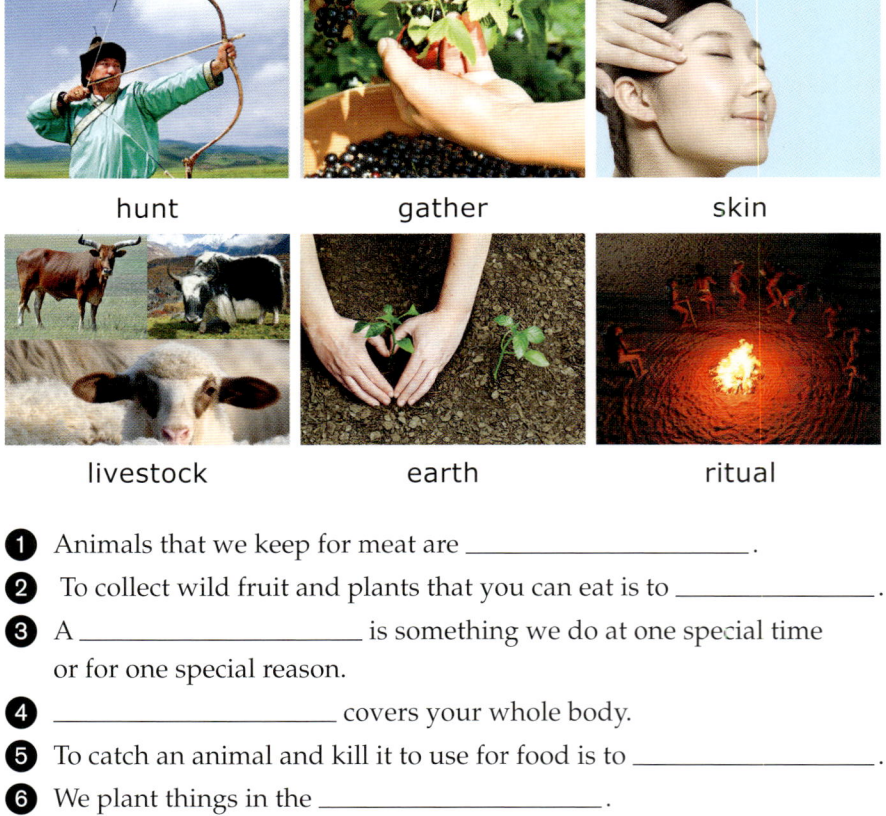

hunt   gather   skin

livestock   earth   ritual

1. Animals that we keep for meat are _____.
2. To collect wild fruit and plants that you can eat is to _____.
3. A _____ is something we do at one special time or for one special reason.
4. _____ covers your whole body.
5. To catch an animal and kill it to use for food is to _____.
6. We plant things in the _____.

Read the text. Then complete the sentences with the correct highlighted words.

The Navajo people in the United States are an example of a tribe. They are a group of people living in the same area with the same way of life. In the past, the Navajo lived in shelters called hogans. These shelters were usually made of wood and covered with wet earth, or mud. The Navajo grew food on their land. They also kept herds of animals for meat.

Today, the Navajo live on their own land in the American southwest. They choose their own leaders who make decisions for the tribe.

1 The part of our planet (the Earth) that is not the ocean is
_____ .

2 Large groups of animals are _____ .

3 Places where you can sleep and eat are _____ .

4 A group of people who live together and have the same daily life is a
_____ .

5 People who make decisions for a group are _____ .

CHAPTER 1

Nomads

UNTIL 10,000 YEARS AGO, ALL PEOPLE ON EARTH WERE NOMADS. TODAY, THERE ARE VERY FEW LEFT.

Today, many people on Earth can get food easily. They can buy it at supermarkets, on street corners, in local stores, from vending machines,[1] and even online. Or they can grow it themselves! But not everyone on Earth can get or grow food that easily. Some people live in remote[2] places or places with very bad weather. To find food to live, they have to be **nomads**.

Today, there are very few nomads. Until 10,000 years ago, however, most people on Earth were hunter-gatherers. Hunter-gatherers move around to find food to eat. During warm weather they stay in one place. They **gather** fruits and vegetables and **hunt** wild animals. When the weather becomes colder, they move to warmer places to find more food.

[1] **vending machine:** a machine that sells food, candy, and drinks

[2] **remote:** far away and difficult to travel to

Pastoral nomads are another kind of nomadic group. Pastoral nomads don't hunt animals. They have livestock. They drink the milk and eat the meat of these animals, and they use the skin for making clothes and building **shelters**.

Livestock in a pasture

Pastoral nomads move around, too, but not as much as hunter-gatherers. These groups move their livestock to different **pastures** within the area where they live. Some pastoral nomads have a different pasture for each season: spring, summer, winter, and fall. Other pastoral nomads have a pasture for a wet, or rainy, season and a pasture for a dry season.

Pastoral nomads have lived on Earth for a long time – perhaps for as long as 5,000 years!

? ANALYZE

Why don't hunter-gatherers and pastoral nomads live in one place?

The San used bows
and arrows to hunt.

CHAPTER 2

The San

THE SAN OF THE KALAHARI ARE NOMADIC
PEOPLE IN SOUTHERN AFRICA.

The San were the first people to live in the southern part of Africa 20,000 years ago. They were hunter-gatherers. They hunted wild animals with bows and arrows and picked wild fruits and vegetables.

The San lived completely off the land. They followed the same path every year to find food. They knew where the best fruits were in each season. They also knew where the antelope went as the seasons changed. Today, there are many fewer San, but they try to live the same life as they did many years ago.

An antelope

The San travel in small groups of about 25 men, women, and children. A few times every year, these groups meet with each other to share news, give presents, and plan marriages.

The San do not have one leader. If there is a problem, or if the group has to decide something, they all decide together. Everyone can share his or her ideas or opinions with the group. The San recognize that they can learn from each other's special experiences.[3] For example, one person in the group may be the best hunter, while another is very good at helping sick people. But no one person has any more power than the others in the group.

Usually it's the men who do the hunting. They hunt in groups and catch antelope, zebras, lions, and snakes, which they cook on a fire. The man who kills the animal gives out the meat to the other people in the group.

---

[3] **experience:** something that happens to you that changes what you know or feel

A snake   A zebra

Sometimes the San gather roots for food.

Roots

When a San boy wants to get married, he hunts a large animal, for example an antelope. Then he takes the best meat to the girl's family and asks her parents if he can marry her. A boy can't get married until he shows that he is a good hunter.

The women usually gather fruits, vegetables, eggs, and wild honey. San women know over 100 kinds of edible[4] plants. They also know which plants you should never eat!

Sometimes, however, men and women need to help each other with their jobs. So, the women help with the hunting, and the men help with the gathering.

In the dry season, it is difficult for the San to find water. Sometimes they have to look for water in the roots of plants. Other times, they dig holes in the sand to look for water.

[4]**edible:** something you can safely eat

For thousands of years, the San lived in peace[6] with the land and each other. Then two thousand years ago, other groups, pastoral nomads and farmers, moved into their area. There was less land for the San.

Then about 350 years ago, white people came to live in southern Africa. They had horses and **guns**. They killed many of the San and stole their land.

Today there are about 100,000 San, but their way of life is in danger. They have less and less land. Many people study them because the San still live very much like the first people on Earth. Some people around the world want to help the San to keep their land and their traditions. They want the San to live the same way they have lived for many thousands of years.

....

[5] **religious:** having a strong belief about God or gods
[6] **peace:** when people get along

CHAPTER 3

The Khanty Tribe

THE KHANTY TRIBE LIVES IN SIBERIA, RUSSIA. THEY HAVE LIVED IN THIS VERY COLD PLACE SINCE THE 1ST CENTURY CE.

In the Siberian *taiga*, or forest, the temperature can be –68° Celsius. Very few plants can grow there. Because of this, the Khanty must hunt and fish for most of their food. There are a few different Khanty groups, but all of them hunt and fish and move from place to place as the seasons change. All the groups make almost everything they use: their homes, their clothes, and even their small boats.

In the south of the Khanty's homeland, some Khanty groups fish, hunt, and eat wild fruits. They sell some of their meat and skins to make money. With the money, they buy a few things like flour to make bread, tea, and sugar. Other southern Khanty groups grow some of their own food, for example vegetables.

A Khanty chum, or tent house

Khanty people with herds of reindeer

?

ANALYZE

Why are the lives of the different Khanty groups different?

The northern Khanty live in large family groups and keep **herds** of reindeer. Each person in the family helps look after the animals. The reindeer give the Khanty food to eat and skins for their clothes. The Khanty move from place to place with their reindeer as the weather changes to find good pastures all year long. This means the reindeer can eat lots of grass and get bigger. They breed[7] and so their herd gets bigger, too.

The Khanty move to the same places at the same times each year. When they move their reindeer herds, they often stay in *chums* – small shelters made from reindeer skins. The chums are like tents. They're easy to put up and take down. When the Khanty must stay in one place for a longer time, they make small wooden houses.

[7]**breed:** make baby animals

The Khanty must keep their reindeer safe from bears. But to the Khanty, the bear is a special, sacred[8] animal. If they must kill a bear, they feel bad about it, so they do a special **ritual**. This ritual makes peace between the bear's spirit[9] and the hunter's spirit. During these rituals, the Khanty eat large meals and dance.

The Khanty believe that the land they live on and the rivers they fish in belong to them. They never bought the land or the rivers, but that doesn't matter. The Khanty believe that they are the descendants of gods and that gods made the land and the rivers and then gave them to the first Khanty people who lived on Earth.

[8]**sacred:** belonging to God or gods
[9]**spirit:** the part of a person or animal that is not the body

Today, the Khanty way of life is in danger. Oil companies have come to look for oil on the Khanty's land. The companies cut down trees and pollute[10] the rivers and lakes. There are fewer fish and animals for the Khanty to hunt. And they have less land for their reindeer herds.

So, today the Khanty must find ways to make money to help them keep their land. Many Khanty families have tourists come to stay with them. These tourists learn about how the Khanty live. The money they pay can help the Khanty save their way of life.

---

[10] **pollute:** make water, land, or air very dirty

Video Quest

Reindeer

Watch this video to learn about the Khanty Tribe of Siberia. Why are the reindeer so important to them?

CHAPTER 4

Mongolian Herders

THE HERDERS OF MONGOLIA ARE AN EXAMPLE OF PASTORAL NOMADS. THEY DON'T HUNT OR FISH. THEY MOVE THEIR LIVESTOCK FROM PASTURE TO PASTURE.

A yak

For 3,000 years, the Mongolian herders have lived on land called steppes. A steppe is a very, very large area of grass. There are no hills or trees. On a steppe, the earth is not good. You can't grow food, but there is lots of grass for animals to eat. So, the herders have livestock.

A camel

Mongolian herders have five different kinds of livestock. They mainly have sheep, but they also have camels, cows or yaks, goats, and horses. The sheep give milk, meat, skins for shelters, and wool for clothes. The camels also give milk and meat, and they help carry things when the herders move from place to place.

The yaks or cows give meat and leather and milk for yogurt and cheese.

Mongolians ride horses on the steppes.

Herders cut and sell the wool of their goats each spring.

Goats are important because of their special kind of wool, called cashmere. Mongolian cashmere is sold all over the world. The money Mongolian herders make each spring from selling the cashmere helps them live for the rest of the year.

Horses are also very important to the Mongolian herders' way of life. The herders ride the horses to look for new pastures as the seasons change. Mongolian children learn to ride at a very early age. They can all ride a horse as easily as they can walk or run. An old Mongol saying is, "A Mongol without a horse is like a bird without wings."

A wing

The herders milk the female horses. This milk is used to make a very popular drink called *airag*. Mongolians of all ages drink lots of airag every day in the summer.

Putting up a ger

The stove is always in the center of the ger.

Mongolian herders live in a *ger*. It is made of wooden poles[11] and wool. When people get married, their families buy or build them the wooden part as a gift. Then the families work together to make the wool part.

A ger weighs about 200 kilograms, and it only takes a Mongolian family a little more than an hour to put it up or take it down. It is cool in summer and warm in winter.

The inside of the ger is always the same. The door is on the south side; the men's place is in the west part; and the women are in the east part. Important guests and old people go to the north part. The stove is always in the center. Gers have beds along the walls, a low table and chairs for eating, and special chairs in the northern part for guests.

[11]**pole:** a long, thin, round piece of wood

Today, the Mongolian herders' life is more difficult. From 1999 until 2002, the summers in Mongolia were very hot and dry. The Mongolians called this weather *zud*. These summers were followed by very long, cold winters. Because of this bad weather, many of the livestock died. The herders had very little food and very little money. Many of them had to move to the capital city, Ulaanbaatar, to try to find work. But there were few jobs for them.

Today, many herder families are joining together to share their livestock and sell their milk, meat, and wool. In this way, they can work together to keep their way of life.

Video Quest

Folk Songs

Watch this video to learn about traditional Mongolian folk songs. Why are the songs important to the herders?

CHAPTER 5

The Roma

NOT ALL NOMADIC GROUPS LIVE IN JUST ONE AREA. THE ROMA PEOPLE FIRST LIVED IN NORTHERN INDIA, BUT NOW THEY LIVE IN MANY DIFFERENT PARTS OF THE WORLD.

In English, the Roma are usually called gypsies, because people thought they came from Egypt. However, these nomads prefer to be called *Roma*, from *rom*, which means "man" or "husband" in their language.

The Roma traveled to Persia by the year 1000, to southeastern Europe by 1300, and then to western Europe by 1400. By 1950, groups of Roma lived on every continent,[12] except for Antarctica.

The Roma live all over the world and speak the language of the country they live in. However, they can all also speak their own language, which is called Romany.

[12]**continent:** one of the seven main areas of land on Earth such as Asia, Africa, and Europe

It is very difficult to say how many Roma there are in the world because they move around so much. Some people think there are two million; others think there are 14 million or more.

Roma families are often very large. In one home, there is usually a married husband and wife, their unmarried children, their married sons, and the sons' wives and children. The sons' wives learn the ways of their husbands' Roma group and how to take care of a family.

A large family group – or in Romany, a *vitsa* – is part of a larger group called a band. A band can have about 200 Roma. The older Roma in the band often plan marriages with Roma from other bands so that there is a friendly relationship[13] between the bands. In the past, when two people got married, the young man's parents had to pay the parents of the young woman. That doesn't happen as much today.

[13]**relationship:** the way people or groups are towards each other

The leader of each Roma band is called the *voivode*. The other Roma in the band choose the voivode, and he is their leader for the rest of his life. The voivode decides things for the band with other elders[14] and with the *phuri dai*. The phuri dai is a special elder woman in the band. The phuri dai decides things that help make the lives of the other women and girls in the band better.

Helping other people in the band is very important to the Roma. If members of a band hurt someone else in the band, the voivode can order them to leave for a while. When their time is over, there is a party to welcome them back into the band.

Most Roma find jobs they can do while traveling. In the past, Roma men bought and sold horses and helped farmers take care of sick animals. Roma men and women made things to sell.

[14]**elder:** one of the oldest people in a group

Today some Roma work with traveling **circuses** and amusement parks.[15] Others do many different things, including working on farms, repairing cars, and building houses.

Flamenco dancers stamp their feet.

The Roma have always been popular entertainers.[16] Their music is famous everywhere in the world. Flamenco is a Spanish Roma music and dance. Flamenco music is made by people who sing and play guitars. Flamenco dancers stamp their feet to the music.

Today, most Roma travel by cars and trailers instead of caravans and horses. Some Roma, however, don't travel any more. They have decided to live in one place.

[15] **amusement park:** a large park where you can ride on machines and have fun

[16] **entertainer:** someone who sings, dances, or plays music for other people to enjoy

Roma used to travel in caravans.

Today they travel in trailers.

CHAPTER 6

What Do You Think?

WOULD YOU LIKE TO TRAVEL AND LIVE IN DIFFERENT PLACES? SOME PEOPLE DO. THEY ARE MODERN-DAY NOMADS.

In many parts of the world, retired[17] people travel to warmer places during the coldest months. Some go to the same warm place every year. For example, some people from Ontario, Canada, go to the west side of Florida in the United States every winter.

Other retired people sell their houses and get recreational vehicles (RVs), which are like houses on wheels. They travel around all year looking for warmer weather. Some younger people also leave their jobs and travel around in RVs. They visit different places and get jobs such as building homes or selling things on the Internet.

Children in these families can't go to school, so their parents home school them. They teach them subjects like math, science, and reading.

[17] **retired:** not working anymore because you are old

And some modern-day nomads just want to see the world. They don't want to sit inside an office at a computer all day. They don't want to see the same people every day. They want to visit other countries, meet other people, and see how they live. Some of these people write books about their travels. Others blog[18] about

their lives traveling around the world. This way, they share their experiences with others.

Do you want to be a modern-day nomad? If yes, where do you want to go? How will you get there? Who do you want to go with, or do you want to travel alone? What kind of job will you do?

[18]**blog:** write on the Internet often about what you are doing and feeling

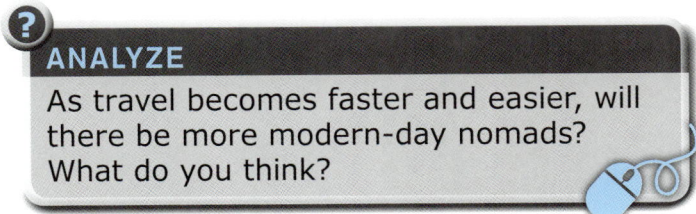

?

ANALYZE

As travel becomes faster and easier, will there be more modern-day nomads? What do you think?

After You Read

True or False

Read the sentences and choose Ⓐ (True) or Ⓑ (False).
If the book does not tell you, choose Ⓒ (Doesn't say).

1 Until 10,000 years ago, some people were pastoral nomads.
Ⓐ True
Ⓑ False
Ⓒ Doesn't say

2 Hunter-gatherers follow wild animals from place to place.
Ⓐ True
Ⓑ False
Ⓒ Doesn't say

3 The San choose a new leader every year.
Ⓐ True
Ⓑ False
Ⓒ Doesn't say

Video

4 The San do the Trance Dance before they gather food.
Ⓐ True
Ⓑ False
Ⓒ Doesn't say

5 Northern Khanty groups have reindeer.
Ⓐ True
Ⓑ False
Ⓒ Doesn't say

6 There are many mountains in the steppes.
Ⓐ True
Ⓑ False
Ⓒ Doesn't say

Match

Match the vocabulary with the correct definitions.

Words	Definitions
1. gather _____	a. a group of people with the same kind of life who live in the same area
2. marry _____	b. the part of Earth that is not ocean
3. livestock _____	c. a person who makes decisions for the group
4. land _____	d. this covers your whole body
5. leader _____	e. animals that we use for meat
6. hunt _____	f. what people do when they want to live together
7. herd _____	g. catch an animal to use it for food
8. shelter _____	h. a place to sleep and eat in
9. tribe _____	i. collect things
10. skin _____	j. a large group of animals

Answer the Questions

Read Chapter 5, pages 20–23, again and answer the questions.

1 What does "rom" mean?

_____

2 Who lives in a Roma family group?

_____

_____

3 What is the most important thing for the Roma?

_____

4 What are the Roma famous for?

_____

_____

Answer Key

Words to Know, page 4
1 livestock **2** gather **3** ritual **4** Skin **5** hunt **6** earth

Words to Know, page 5
1 land **2** herds **3** shelters **4** tribe **5** leaders

Analyze, page 7
They need to move from place to place to find food.

Video Quest, page 11
The San do the Trance Dance before they hunt. They do this dance to talk to the spirits of the natural world.

Analyze, page 13
They live in different places, so their needs are also different.

Video Quest, page 15
The reindeer is their most important food. They also use its skin to make shoes and clothes and shelter.

Video Quest, page 19
The songs tell about Mongolian history.

Analyze, page 25   *Answers will vary.*

True or False, page 26
1 B **2** A **3** B **4** B **5** A **6** B

Match, page 27
1 i **2** f **3** e **4** b **5** c **6** g **7** j **8** h **9** a **10** d

Answer the Questions, page 27
1 "man" or "husband" **2** mother, father, children and married sons and the sons' wives and children **3** to help other Roma **4** music and entertainment